Guided Journal

A LITTLE BIT OF

MEDITATION

Guided Journal

A LITTLE BIT OF

MEDITATION

YOUR PERSONAL PATH
TO MINDFULNESS

AMY LEIGH MERCREE

STERLING ETHOS
New York

THIS BOOK BELONGS TO

STERLING ETHOS
New York

An Imprint of Sterling Publishing Co., Inc.
1166 Avenue of the Americas
New York, NY 10036

ISBN 978-1-4549-4034-0

Distributed in Canada by Sterling Publishing Co., Inc.
c/o Canadian Manda Group, 664 Annette Street
Toronto, Ontario M6S 2C8, Canada
Distributed in the United Kingdom by GMC Distribution Services
Castle Place, 166 High Street, Lewes, East Sussex BN7 1XU, England
Distributed in Australia by NewSouth Books
University of New South Wales, Sydney, NSW 2052, Australia

For information about custom editions, special sales, and premium and corporate purchases,
please contact Sterling Special Sales at 800-805-5489 or specialsales@sterlingpublishing.com.

Manufactured in Singapore

2 4 6 8 10 9 7 5 3 1

sterlingpublishing.com

Cover design by Elizabeth Mihaltse Lindy
Interior design by Sharon Jacobs

Image Credits:
Fuzzimo.com: cover; Shutterstock: Kittikiti: cover, throughout; satit_srihin: cover, throughout

❧ CONTENTS ☙

INTRODUCTION ix

❧ 1 ☙ DIFFERENT MEDITATION STYLES 1

❧ 2 ☙ MEDITATIONS TO OPEN HEART & MIND.................... 9

❧ 3 ☙ GUIDED MEDITATION TO OPEN YOUR HEART 17

❧ 4 ☙ OM: THE UNIVERSAL SOUND.............................. 37

❧ 5 ☙ YOUR INNER WITNESS..................................... 45

CONCLUSION 55

ACKNOWLEDGMENTS......................................180

ABOUT THE AUTHOR.......................................181

INTRODUCTION

In our culture, many roads lead to the art and cultivation of mindfulness. When people seek treatment for anxiety, meditation is often recommended. As people learn meditation, mindfulness is a result. Being conscious to and present in the moment to the exclusion of almost everything else enables us to be happier and healthier.

The idea of "consciousness" has been gaining popularity since the 1960s in the Western world. Consciousness in this context is the infinite awareness of being, within us all. It is the witnessing part of the self that is always in the background observing life around us. Meditation, in its many forms, cultivates awareness of consciousness.

In *A Little Bit of Meditation Guided Journal*, we explore the history of the practice of meditation and its origins, and learn practical applications of how to bring conscious awareness into daily life to improve the quality of our experience on earth. We will discuss the physical, emotional, mental, and spiritual ramifications of meditating in daily life. A wide variety of practical activities and meditations are included. So, dive in and find your center!

THIS JOURNAL

Join me and indulge in a relaxing little bit of meditation. This journal will guide you on a path to peace and greater awareness. It can be used on its own, or in conjunction with *A Little Bit of Meditation*, which includes more in-depth information on some of the material in this book.

DIFFERENT MEDITATION STYLES

Hinduism

Meditation in Hinduism developed out of early Vedic texts, and later, the Upanishads. The earliest forms of meditation were focused on trying to understand ultimate reality. Is the universe a projection of humanity, or is humanity a projection of the universe? Is the universe an illusion, or is our individual existence an illusion?

Scholars of early Hinduism are aware of four types of meditation based on the ancient texts. Rishis were ancient seers or sages who took what they learned from meditation and composed hymns about their conclusions. They wrote of mantra meditation, visual meditation, meditation on learned insights in the heart and mind, and, finally, an ecstatic state that occurs when merging with the universal reality of Brahman (divinity). Early Hinduism also had ascetic adherents who incorporated various other practices such as breath control and the ability to levitate. Similar descriptions of ascetic shaman-seers have been included in modern-day writings like *Autobiography of a Yogi* by Paramahansa Yogananda.

Hindu meditation developed over the centuries as a multifaceted approach to self-realization called Yoga Vedanta. The yogic path includes components such as service, knowledge, and devotion, and is variable according to each individual's needs. Because Hinduism dates back thousands of years, many schools of thought have risen from it with nuanced differences in belief and practice.

Buddhism

Buddhism developed in India out of early Hinduism. Unlike the yogic eight-limb path—eight guidelines to living a meaningful and purposeful life as outlined by the sage Patanjali—Buddhism emphasizes three "trainings." Many Americans are most familiar with just the meditation training. However, the other two trainings, wisdom and ethics, are considered to be interconnected with the practice of meditation. Following the death of the Buddha, several doctrinal canons emerged with his supposed teachings. There remains scholarly debate on the authenticity of various portions of these canons, which helped give rise to the different schools of Buddhism.

With the Silk Road—an ancient network of routes that connected distant regions of the Asian continent—opening up trade during the Middle Ages, Buddhist meditation teachings were transmitted out of India and throughout Eastern Asia. Around the eighth century, they spread to Japan in the form of Zen. The primary schools of Buddhism that were cemented over time are Mahayana, Theravada, Pure Land, Zen, and Vajrayana. Each school developed its own meditation practices.

Judaism

A current of meditation practices has run through Judaism for centuries. As one writer put it, meditation is so wrapped up in the daily rituals of Jewish life that they weren't separated out as individual practices. However, the rituals gave many moments for "meditative awareness," even if they weren't specifically called meditation.

Many of the more technical types of Jewish meditation were recorded as oral traditions, especially in the mystical Kabbalah literature, so they may not have permeated out to the mainstream Jewish population. However, there were many Hebrew words that would have been familiar to lay practitioners that implicitly described various forms of meditation practices such as seclusion, focused concentration, and visualization.

Christianity

Early Christianity is known for its Desert Fathers and Mothers, ascetics and monks who went out into the wilderness to seclude themselves and commune with God. Early Common Era writings from some of these ascetics point to the practice of mantra meditation, calling it "pure prayer." In the Middle Ages following the East-West Schism in Christianity, the practices of Lectio Divina (a meditative reading of Scripture) and hesychasm (a meditation based on repetition of the Jesus Prayer) developed and took root. Over the centuries, meditative practices remained within various contemplative branches of Christianity, especially within monastic communities. However, they are experiencing a resurgence of popularity within the mainstream Christian population.

Islam

The bulk of meditation practices in early Islam came through the mystical branch of Sufism. Two early forms, practiced as early as the fourth century AD, were silent dhikr (rhythmic repetition of God's names and attributes) and the meditation of the heart. The motivation behind both of these practices is the intense energy of love, both toward others and toward God. By focusing on love, thoughts and emotions will fade away.

Sufis are most known for the meditative practice of "whirling." Sufi orders were first established in the twelfth century, and many took part in this activity. Whirling is a physical meditation that helps one connect with God through music, movement, and the relinquishment of ego and individual desires. Though whirling is most identified with Sufism, there are several other orders of Sufism and meditation practices as well. One order, started in the fourteenth century, is called the Silent Sufis. They believe that God must be reached only in silence.

Your meditation practice can be as regimented or as spontaneous as you would like. It is for you! What resonates with you about each of the listed religions or philosophies, or any others? Which aspects of each philosophy stand out to you? Do you feel inspired by specific ideas of each way of thinking and feeling?

Hinduism

Buddhism

Judaism

Christianity

Journal your experiences integrating different aspects of world philosophies. As you connected with Sufism and music, how did you feel? When you reflect upon Buddhism, does it resonate for you that it is actually a philosophy, not a religion? What might you like about that? Try meditating and connecting with the essence of these various world religions/philosophies and contemplate the experiences here in your journal.

2

MEDITATIONS TO OPEN HEART & MIND

MEDITATION IS THE PROCESS OF ENTERING INTO a receptive state and letting the goodness of the universe fill you. It is dipping your toe into a pool of infinite stillness. Open your mind and heart to the idea that meditation can transform you. It is not a flashy cleanse or a trendy detox. Meditation offers an open door to a more balanced and centered lifestyle. It permeates your whole being. Your state of mind and clarity of thinking will improve. Your heart and emotions will heal and open gently. Your body will produce fewer stress hormones and improve in health. And, your spirit will relax and learn to witness itself—the first step to enlightenment.

In deep meditation, people sometimes experience the powerful phenomenon of surrender. When we surrender in a spiritual sense, we let go of all effort and strain and become open to receive. Sometimes we feel spontaneous bursts of forgiveness toward others and ourselves. Meditation can open the door and welcome all the unfathomably vast goodness in the universe.

What does the idea of surrender mean to you?

What about being receptive?

What might a deep state of openness and receptivity feel like?

How could surrendering to your own inner light and trusting it help you open your heart?

Do you get a sense that surrender and openness could help you forgive those who have wronged you?

What about forgiving yourself?

How might forgiveness open the door to new levels of authenticity and even self-love?

❖ 3 ❖

GUIDED MEDITATION TO OPEN YOUR HEART

WHEN DISCUSSING THE IDEA OF THE "INNER witness"—the eternally calm, infinite part of yourself—you might not suspect that the next logical step is a conversation about having an open heart. The inner witness is in fact a big part of having an expansive and open emotional center. In meditation, that's the meaning behind the saying, "an open heart." Having an open heart obviously means not closing your heart, and that sounds easy, right? Well, it's actually pretty challenging to maintain.

Every day, we have experiences that might lead us to close our hearts. We feel self-conscious, or we doubt ourselves. Somebody gets mad at us, or we get mad at ourselves because of a decision we made. We are human, and, by definition, that means we are not perfect. We are unique and quirky, and we have weaknesses and strengths. And we're diverse. A situation that hurts my feelings and makes me feel like crying might make someone else really mad and want to get in a fistfight, and still another person might not even be affected by it. As human beings, our diversity can be our strength.

We can all find spiritual growth and fulfillment and ultimately experience less suffering in the endeavor to keep an open heart. Our emotional selves are like a field of constantly moving and flowing energy. The energy moves around and through the body and is anchored at the center of the chest, which some people call the heart chakra. It is one of the main emotional centers. This is a place where emotional energy flows in and out of the body.

When we feel hurt or slighted, that area sometimes constricts. But what if we are able to keep it open and expansive all the time? In the book *The Untethered Soul: The Journey Beyond Yourself*, Michael A. Singer talks about the concept of "samskaras." Samskaras are the impressions of stored energy that are left when we close the heart instead of keeping it open. If we allow an experience—good or bad— to just pass through the body instead of grasping at it or having an aversion to it (which closes the heart), and instead keep the heart open, then we do not create a samskara.

Let's practice!

Sit or lie down somewhere comfortable, where you will be undisturbed for about fifteen or twenty minutes. Find a relaxed posture and follow your breath for a few minutes. Let your mind calm down.

Now bring your attention to the center of your chest. Notice what it feels like. Does it already feel open and expansive? Does it feel partially constricted? You can bring your hands up to massage the area physically; use a dragging motion across the skin, as if you are pulling your hands to the side and opening your chest. Envision opening, relaxing, and expanding and think about the feeling of love. If you would like to use an essential oil, you can mix a rose essential oil with a carrier oil (used to dilute the essential oil), then rub a small amount into the area and inhale the aroma. (Make sure to apply the oil on a small patch of skin first, to test for any adverse reactions, before liberally applying.)

If your heart center feels especially constricted, you can use eucalyptus oil (mixed with a carrier oil). This will bring invigorating energy to the area. Sometimes when the area has been constricted for too long, it becomes lethargic or shuts down. In that case, we need to wake it up, but gently, so as not to shake free too many samskaras at once. Ideally, you just want to engage in a gentle process of heart healing that will only enhance your life and not disrupt it. Take your time. There's no rush.

In your relaxed position, keep breathing. Breathe into the center of your chest and really feel it expand on the inhale. Anything that is not love or light will be easily exhaled and released. Breathe more and more deeply each time. As you reach a relaxed state, close your eyes and continue breathing. Let yourself surrender to the sensation. Simply stay open. Let any positive or negative emotions, memories, colors, sounds, or sensations pass through you. Don't grasp at them or attempt to observe them as they pass.

Engage in this heart breathing for as long as you'd like. You can continue to massage your chest, as needed. Keep opening and relaxing your chest. Relax your neck. Relax your shoulders, arms, and hands, feeling the heart-based relaxation ripple through your body.

When the exercise feels complete, you can slowly bring your attention back into the room. Vigorously rub your arms and legs. Make sure you feel fully present to yourself. You can state the words "I am here" over and over if you so please.

After you complete this exercise, it's a great idea to drink water with a tiny pinch of unprocessed Himalayan or Hawaiian salt. Celtic sea salt also works wonderfully. This helps flush out any toxins that were released during the meditation. When you get rid of emotional toxicity, the body responds by releasing physical toxins from storage zones in fat cells in the body. So it's important to flush it out.

I also advise that you engage in some vigorous physical exercise after this. If you only have a few minutes, do a set of thirty jumping jacks or anything that will help you break a sweat and start moving energy. When you meditate to open your heart and clear it, you also engage in powerful physical detoxification.

One of the states we are cultivating when we meditate is nonattachment. Part of nonattachment is to not grasp our experiences too tightly or push them away. Instead, we allow ourselves a bit of emotional distance, especially when we feel triggered by life's events. Attachment is what creates samskaras or densities that we have held on to too tightly. After doing this meditation, do you feel like you got a sense of what nonattachment feels like? How did you experience it? What areas of your life might benefit from a bit of it?

Can you think of situations or times in your life where you might have held on too tightly to an unpleasant experience?

You can practice the meditation we just did (pages 18-20) to help release those densities, focusing on relaxing and opening your heart. Surrendering to the peace of your meditation and the inner witness within you will allow this. Make any notes below about how you have experienced that thus far.

Are there moments in your life to which you have clung because they were so positive?

That is beautiful and part of how we form our self-concept and enjoy life.

Identify those peak experiences here. List some.

You can embrace those moments and also allow yourself to not grip them too tightly, instead, being with the present and magnetizing more positive experiences to yourself now and in the future. Do this by meditating with a mantra like:

**"LIFE IS JOYFUL AND EASY FOR ME.
I ALLOW MYSELF TO ATTRACT
SPECTACULAR EXPERIENCES!"**

Repeat this affirmation a few times during a meditation and throughout the day to relax into attracting serendipity to your life through nonattachment and surrender.

How does your life feel changed by this meditation practice?

"I choose to flow
with life and
let go into goodness."

What might flowing with life feel like? How might your behavior change
if you did this?

"I open into feeling and being,
letting my receptivity
magnetize my heart's desires."

The opposite of feeling and being is thinking and doing. One is receptive; one is active. Do you think your responses are more active or receptive? Reflect on why that might be.

"When I mediate,
I allow myself to become
a benevolent observer
of myself."

How does it feel when you mediate and view yourself with nonattachment? Do you sense a lightness, a benevolence in your deepest being?

"I trust in life.

I know in my soul that all

is right in the world."

When we let go of attachment during meditation, we are able to sense that our lives are in the flow, however they appear. After you meditate, do you view your life differently? Are you more aligned with your soul's life plan?

4

OM:
THE UNIVERSAL
SOUND

IF YOU LOOK AT THE CREATION OF THE EARTH, you'll see that all the forces of physics combined to create an ebb and flow that keeps everything running in a continuous, harmonious circle of life. Like a well-oiled machine, we've all been connected since the beginning of time through a beautiful, mystical process of unity. And, since the beginning, we've all been dancing to the beat of one certain drum—a vibration, really. If we were to put that very vibration into a word, it would simply be om, a universal sound respected by all religions and uttered by many reflective souls.

Om, written in Hindu as "*aum*," is the most sacred sound and the most recognized symbol in Hinduism. It represents the infinite energy of divinity and depicts how we can all live in a world of harmony. Known by some as the primordial vibration of the entire universe, including ourselves, it provides a space for all of philosophy and mythology to meet and dwell together. In fact, it precedes and ends almost every Hindu incantation or mantra. The universal sound of om has been found in manuscripts and writings since the creation of the Vedic traditions of Hinduism, Jainism, and Buddhism. According to the *International Journal of Yoga*, the descriptions of om have been taken from four Upanishads (*Mundaka*, *Mandukya*, *Svetasvatara*, and *Katha*), the *Bhagavad Gita*, and Patanjali's *Yoga Sutras*. In Christianity, om is the start of omega, the beginning and the end, and can also be found in the word *amen*. The Indian scriptures regard the sacred syllable om as the primordial sound from which all other sounds emerge, which signifies om as the Supreme Power.

Om is the expression of all the sounds in the universe and, repeated, blends to form a perfect continuous humming. How does this work? Earth's physics help keep everything moving in a continuous circle—up and down, right and left, rinse and repeat—and the sound of *om* is structured the same way. The om meditation consists of three letters (*A*, *U*, and *M*) that cover the entire scope of the way we've learned to articulate through spoken language. *Om* as *aum* is actually structured by four sounds. The *A* sound comes from your throat but starts in your stomach. The *U* originates in the chest and requires the help of the tongue. The *M* sound stems from your head and comes out through a vibration in your lips. The last sound is merely silence, when the lungs have run out of air but the word still lingers on the body. *Om* is natural for you to say because it consists of every sound you ever learned to make as a child. The beginning *A*—when the sound originates in the stomach area—is representative of the creation of all humanity. The *U* represents the ability for your body to breathe in new life and preserve the life you currently lead. The *M* shows that all change must first happen in the mind. The silence is representative of the stillness that brings about reformation and salvation.

With roots in mythology and also ties to the Trimurti (the trinity) in Hinduism, the *aum* sound is also representative: The *A* is Brahma's golden nucleus; the *U* is Vishnu, who was holding Brahma on a lotus, just as your torso sustains your head; and the *M* is the final cycle of existence.

There are plenty of benefits to be had by correctly practicing the mantra of *om*. Studies concerning autonomic and respiratory processes show that while the mind concentrates on the *om* meditation, the body is combining mental alertness with physiological rest. This can help neurons in the brain have a clear path for processing. Meditation has also been proven to slow the heart rate and calm breathing. Chanting om reduces stress and boosts relaxation. A study performed at Lady Irwin College in New Delhi says chanting *om* can help athletes predict dehydration, meaning awareness of their bodily functions improves thanks to the sensitivity that comes from *om*.

This can be said with certainty about *om:* It is a universal sound that is representative of the unity that's needed to empathize with those around us. It's a sound and word that encompasses all of life in a mystical and connected way.

Sit or lie down in a quiet spot. Take a moment to feel your breath moving in and out of your body. Notice the feeling of the air as it comes in your nose or mouth and moves down through your throat into your lungs and then back out again. Just observe the sensations in your body caused by the simple act of breathing. Now, introduce your om mantra. You can say the word internally or aloud. *Om*. Repeat it slowly and with attention. You can say it in a repetitive manner, if that feels good. Or, you can just say it a few times as you observe your breathing. When you say the word *om* out loud, allow yourself to really stretch it out and feel the vibratory frequency in your mouth and throat. Do this as many times as feels good to you. Notice any sensations in your body.

What did repeating *om* feel like?

Did you physically feel the vibration of the word in your mouth, teeth, throat, or face as you said it?

What did you notice as you were observing your breathing?

YOUR INNER
WITNESS

THE INNER MONOLOGUE VOICE. WE ALL HAVE IT. It's that nagging voice that's always chattering away inside your head. It's the same voice that is saying the words you are reading right now so that it feels like you are hearing them in your head. How many times per day does that voice ask or say something to distract you from what is actually happening in your life in the present moment?

I should go to the gym.
I'm getting so lazy.
Why hasn't he called me back?
He must not like me anymore.
I don't know why I bother doing this work.
It doesn't mean anything.

That inner voice can talk us through difficult situations. It can help us make the list that we need to have a successful day. It can help us navigate subtle emotional nuances with our friends and family. It is our "personality self." It's the part of us that's in the forefront, thinking and doing.

In *The Untethered Soul*, this phenomenon of mind chatter taking control of your life is known as your "inner roommate." The inner roommate lives in your head, dictating your thoughts, your reactions, and your emotional state. How do we turn down the volume on this inner chatter? How do we rise out of the negative thinking that our mind chatter can feed? Who is responsible for this mind chatter, anyway? Is it you? Is the inner voice who you are?

The external world plays a massive part on the influence of the chatter in our mind. Between what we are receiving through social interactions and consumption of all kinds of media, our inner monologue is constantly being fed and thrives off persistent stimulation. So much of what we see and hear from the media tells us that who we are simply isn't good enough. This couldn't be further from the truth! We are all beautiful expressions of creative and benevolent universal energy.

This isn't to say that we don't have any issues. We all have problems, some of which are more serious. But some of these problems are simple parts of human existence that get inflated through the cycle of listening to our chaotic inner thoughts.

BECOMING YOUR INNER WITNESS

The problem with the inner roommate is that we tend to think that, because it's in our head, living within us, it's a part of us. But what if we could picture that inner roommate as an actual entity outside our bodies? Thinking of the inner roommate as separate from ourselves is the first step in shifting our awareness into a deeper conscious state. As we move to the state of witnessing the object of disturbance rather than *being* the object of disturbance, we create an objective awareness. This creation allows us to separate our selves from this mental disturbance.

That's not to say that the problems you experience will disappear. They will continue to exist. But as you create this division and develop objectivity toward what you are witnessing, you can control its level of influence on your thoughts and start to move toward a place of inner peace. When you rewire your consciousness to see things for what they really are, rather than seeing them with a false lens influenced by outside factors, you allow yourself to bear witness. As you bear witness, you can move to a different frame of reference with ease and discernment rather than get involved with what the thoughts are saying. You can move into a place of responsibility and ownership rather than getting lost in the vortex of the problem itself.

As you sit in meditation, allow yourself to relax more deeply and let the mind chatter fall away. Then, if you just sit back into yourself a little bit, you can begin to feel what's behind the personality self. Relax your heart and try to sense that behind all of the mind chatter is your silent, inner-witness presence. It is pure peace, and it is your divine soul— your highest self. It is eternally present. It is the part of you that existed before entering the body you currently inhabit, and it will exist after you exit that body. This is your inner witness.

What qualities does your inner roommate have?

Is your inner roommate helpful, neurotic, obsessed with certain topics?
Describe her here.

When you sit back into yourself and rest into the presence of your inner

witness, what changes in the way you think and feel?

What qualities does your inner witness seem to have?

When you are present to your inner witness, and you tap into its depth and vastness for a moment, what adjectives would you use to describe the experience and the way that it feels in your body and your consciousness?

CONCLUSION

EMEMBER, THERE IS A QUIET, GENTLE WITNESS inside of you, lovingly watching everything you do and simply being present to your magnificence. You are a soul and spirit incarnated in a physical form and there are myriad tools available to you to ease the journey and make it worthwhile. Meditation is one of those great tools. Use it. Use the following pages to journal about your own meditation practice. Think of this journal as a space safe to neutrally explore what comes up when you try the exercises suggested in it. Good luck!

XO,

Amy

DATE | TIME

MINDSET BEFORE MEDITATION

MINDSET AFTER MEDITATION

DATE | TIME

MINDSET BEFORE MEDITATION

MINDSET AFTER MEDITATION

DATE | TIME

MINDSET BEFORE MEDITATION

MINDSET AFTER MEDITATION

DATE | TIME

MINDSET BEFORE MEDITATION

MINDSET AFTER MEDITATION

DATE | TIME

MINDSET BEFORE MEDITATION

MINDSET AFTER MEDITATION

DATE | TIME

MINDSET BEFORE MEDITATION

MINDSET AFTER MEDITATION

DATE | TIME

MINDSET BEFORE MEDITATION

MINDSET AFTER MEDITATION

DATE | TIME

MINDSET BEFORE MEDITATION

MINDSET AFTER MEDITATION

DATE | TIME

MINDSET BEFORE MEDITATION

MINDSET AFTER MEDITATION

DATE | TIME

MINDSET BEFORE MEDITATION

MINDSET AFTER MEDITATION

DATE | TIME

MINDSET BEFORE MEDITATION

MINDSET AFTER MEDITATION

DATE | TIME

MINDSET BEFORE MEDITATION

MINDSET AFTER MEDITATION

DATE | **TIME**

MINDSET BEFORE MEDITATION

MINDSET AFTER MEDITATION

DATE | TIME

MINDSET BEFORE MEDITATION

MINDSET AFTER MEDITATION

DATE | TIME

MINDSET BEFORE MEDITATION

MINDSET AFTER MEDITATION

DATE | TIME

MINDSET BEFORE MEDITATION

MINDSET AFTER MEDITATION

DATE | TIME

MINDSET BEFORE MEDITATION

MINDSET AFTER MEDITATION

DATE   TIME

MINDSET BEFORE MEDITATION

MINDSET AFTER MEDITATION

DATE | TIME

MINDSET BEFORE MEDITATION

MINDSET AFTER MEDITATION

DATE | TIME

MINDSET BEFORE MEDITATION

MINDSET AFTER MEDITATION

MINDSET BEFORE MEDITATION

MINDSET AFTER MEDITATION

DATE | TIME

MINDSET BEFORE MEDITATION

MINDSET AFTER MEDITATION

MINDSET BEFORE MEDITATION

MINDSET AFTER MEDITATION

DATE | TIME

MINDSET BEFORE MEDITATION

MINDSET AFTER MEDITATION

DATE | TIME

MINDSET BEFORE MEDITATION

MINDSET AFTER MEDITATION

DATE | TIME |

MINDSET BEFORE MEDITATION

MINDSET AFTER MEDITATION

DATE | TIME

MINDSET BEFORE MEDITATION

MINDSET AFTER MEDITATION

DATE | TIME

MINDSET BEFORE MEDITATION

MINDSET AFTER MEDITATION

DATE | TIME

MINDSET BEFORE MEDITATION

MINDSET AFTER MEDITATION

DATE | TIME

MINDSET BEFORE MEDITATION

MINDSET AFTER MEDITATION

MINDSET BEFORE MEDITATION

MINDSET AFTER MEDITATION

DATE | TIME

MINDSET BEFORE MEDITATION

MINDSET AFTER MEDITATION

DATE | TIME

MINDSET BEFORE MEDITATION

MINDSET AFTER MEDITATION

DATE | TIME

MINDSET BEFORE MEDITATION

MINDSET AFTER MEDITATION

MINDSET BEFORE MEDITATION

MINDSET AFTER MEDITATION

DATE | TIME

MINDSET BEFORE MEDITATION

MINDSET AFTER MEDITATION

MINDSET BEFORE MEDITATION

MINDSET AFTER MEDITATION

DATE | TIME

MINDSET BEFORE MEDITATION

MINDSET AFTER MEDITATION

MINDSET BEFORE MEDITATION

MINDSET AFTER MEDITATION

MINDSET BEFORE MEDITATION

MINDSET AFTER MEDITATION

DATE | TIME

MINDSET BEFORE MEDITATION

MINDSET AFTER MEDITATION

DATE | TIME

MINDSET BEFORE MEDITATION

MINDSET AFTER MEDITATION

DATE | TIME

MINDSET BEFORE MEDITATION

MINDSET AFTER MEDITATION

MINDSET BEFORE MEDITATION

MINDSET AFTER MEDITATION

DATE | TIME

MINDSET BEFORE MEDITATION

MINDSET AFTER MEDITATION

DATE | TIME |

MINDSET BEFORE MEDITATION

MINDSET AFTER MEDITATION

MINDSET BEFORE MEDITATION

MINDSET AFTER MEDITATION

DATE | TIME

MINDSET BEFORE MEDITATION

MINDSET AFTER MEDITATION

DATE | TIME

MINDSET BEFORE MEDITATION

MINDSET AFTER MEDITATION

DATE | TIME

MINDSET BEFORE MEDITATION

MINDSET AFTER MEDITATION

MINDSET BEFORE MEDITATION

MINDSET AFTER MEDITATION

MINDSET BEFORE MEDITATION

MINDSET AFTER MEDITATION

DATE   TIME

MINDSET BEFORE MEDITATION

MINDSET AFTER MEDITATION

DATE | TIME

MINDSET BEFORE MEDITATION

MINDSET AFTER MEDITATION

DATE | TIME

MINDSET BEFORE MEDITATION

MINDSET AFTER MEDITATION

DATE | TIME

MINDSET BEFORE MEDITATION

MINDSET AFTER MEDITATION

ACKNOWLEDGMENTS

Thanks so much to the talented team at Sterling. It is wonderful to collaborate once again! Kate Zimmermann has been a gift and a blessing in my life and career. She has a knack for bringing forth books and journals that share deep truths and resonate with readers. Thanks so much to the talented designers, Elizabeth Lindy and Sharon Jacobs, who made this journal so lovely. The sales, distribution, and marketing teams at Sterling are some of the absolute best in the business. I feel such gratitude when I see one of my books in Whole Foods, Francesca's, Good Earth Trading, or any of the other amazing stores within which you place them.

My incredible agent, Lisa Hagan, has made my dreams come true for ten years. I am so lucky to have her in my corner.

ABOUT THE AUTHOR

Amy Leigh Mercree is a best-selling author, holistic health expert, and medical intuitive. Mercree speaks and teaches internationally, sharing Next Level Healing, Meet Your Guides, Mindfulness Meditation, and Bestseller Bootcamp classes.

Mercree is the author of *The Spiritual Girl's Guide to Dating*, *A Little Bit of Chakras*, *Joyful Living: 101 Ways to Transform Your Spirit & Revitalize Your Life*, *The Chakras and Crystals Cookbook*, *The Compassion Revolution: 30 Days of Living from the Heart*, *A Little Bit of Meditation*, *Essential Oils Handbook*, *Apple Cider Vinegar Handbook*, *A Little Bit of Mindfulness*, *The Mood Book*, *A Little Bit of Goddess*, and *100 Days to Calm*.

Mercree has been featured in *Glamour* magazine; *Women's Health, Inc.* magazine; *Shape*; *The Huffington Post*; *Your Tango*; *Soul and Spirit* magazine; *Mind Body Green*; *Hello Giggles*; *Reader's Digest*; *O, The Oprah Magazine*; *Forbes*; *First for Women*; *Country Living*; *Bustle*; *Elite Daily*; *Thrive Global*; CBS; NBC; FOX; and many more.

Mercree is fast becoming one of the most quoted women on the web. See what all the buzz is about @AmyLeighMercree on social media.